THE GLITCH FORCE BOOK #1

ATTACK OF THE KILLER BUNNIES

AN UNOFFICIAL GRAPHIC NOVEL FOR MINECRAFTERS

MEGAN MILLER

SKY PONY PRESS
New York

Published in the UK by Scholastic, 2023
1 London Bridge, London, SE1 9BG
Scholastic Ireland, 89E Lagan Road, Dublin Industrial Estate, Glasnevin, Dublin, D11 HP5F

SCHOLASTIC and associated logos are trademarks and/or registered trademarks of Scholastic Inc.

Originally published in the US by Sky Pony Press, an imprint of Skyhorse Publishing, Inc., 2022

Cover design by Kai Texel
Cover and interior art by Megan Miller

ISBN 978 07023 3135 0

A CIP catalogue record for this book is available from the British Library.

Printed in Great Britain by Bell and Bain Ltd, Glasgow

Paper made from wood grown in sustainable forests and other controlled sources.

1 3 5 7 9 10 8 6 4 2

This is a work of fiction. Names, characters, places incidents and dialogues are products of the author's imagination or are used fictitiously. Any resemblance to actual people, living or dead, events or locales is entirely coincidental.

www.scholastic.co.uk

INTRODUCTION

Imagine that your mother is a quantum electronics researcher with an experimental lab in your basement, and she leaves the key to the lab in a really obvious spot. You might want to sneak down to the lab at night and start playing around with the equipment. You might learn a massive amount about experimental electronics. You might even make a radical discovery while you are messing around with the programming code of your favourite game, VR technology and some nifty quantum electro-tube gizmos. A radical discovery that lets you and your two best friends enter right into your favourite game. I don't have to imagine, because I'm Duncan and this is exactly what happened to me.

MEET THE GLITCH FORCE

DUNCAN

A genius redstoner who can't resist testing out the quantum electronic gizmos in his mother's research lab.

MIRANDA

A sharpshooter with encyclopedic knowledge of Minecraft.

ZED

An expert builder with a prankster heart.

Chapter 1:
Anomaly

These things are everywhere!

Look – there's a house! let's go in.

Phew.

Um. I'm not sure this was the best choice.

We're in a woodland mansion...

...home of the evoker.

CHAPTER 2: EVOKER

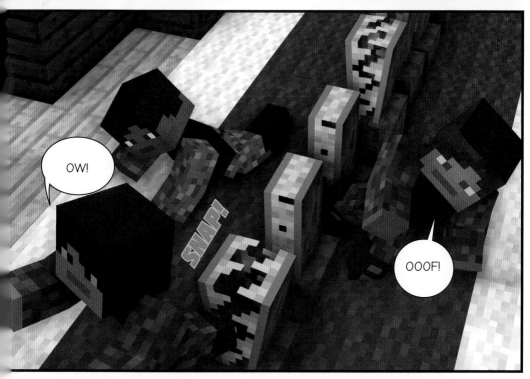

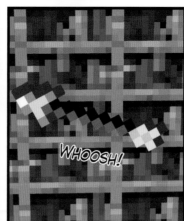

CHAPTER 3:
WOOL

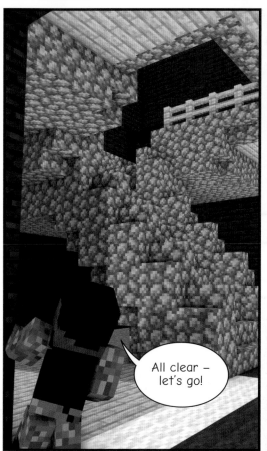

All clear – let's go!

Now which way?

These mansions are randomly generated, so the next stairs could be in either direction.

Let's go this way.

The staircase to the next floor is in its own room.

CLOMP!

CLOMP!

What's that?

Someone's coming! In here!

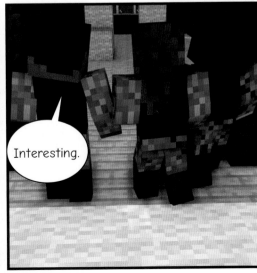

Chapter 4: Loot

We can get weapons. Some of these mansion rooms have chests with great loot. I know all the loot rooms.

So what do we do?

Hopefully the evokers are sleeping. If so, we can search the ground floor, and maybe the next floor, to get whatever loot and weapons we can find.

Then we attack. Let's go!

What kind of rooms are we looking for?

A room with a boxing ring. A bedroom with a loft. A room with fences on the walls. A diagonal wall with a wooden staircase on the side. A stair that goes nowhere. A room with dark oak arches.

How about a weird tree room?

Nope.

Here, have a diamond sword! And an axe! And string! And an iron bucket.

String, please. I can make a bow.

Take it all and let's keep going!

A little later...

We've cleared the ground floor. Time to search the second floor.

Here's another loot room. The ches is up there, above the door.

Another diamond sword and a golden apple. Redstone dust. An enchanted bow. So much stuff!

Take it all.

We've scoured both floors without running into one illager. Let's go to the third floor. We passed the stai room a little while back.

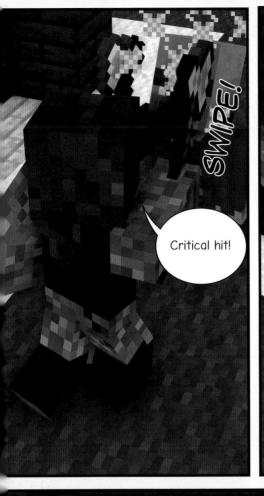

CHAPTER 5:
BACK TO THE
BEGINNING

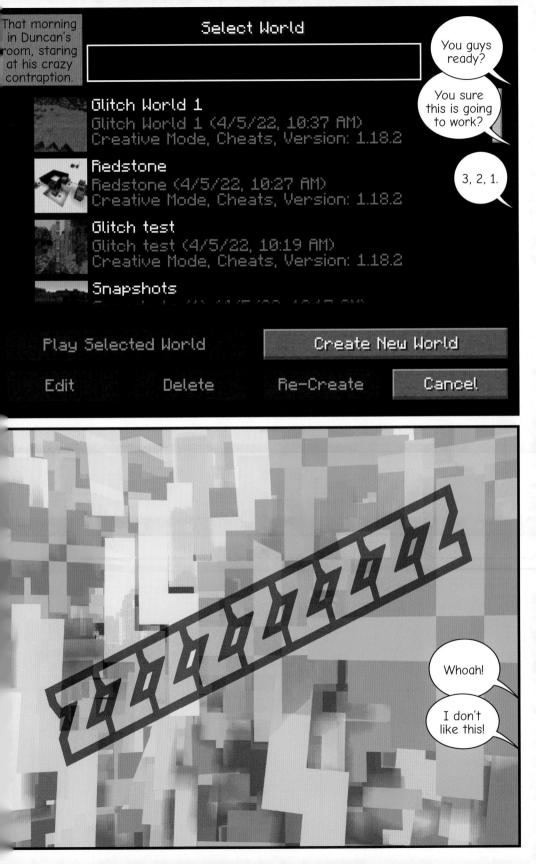

Whooo!

I'm so fast!

And now I'm not. I can't run anymore.

We forgot food.

We need to kill sheep for wool to make beds and then eat the mutton.

Look. There are sheep over there.

I don't know about this. Maybe we can find some potatoes?

It's okay. They're just made of pixels. They're not real sheep. Even if it feels real, we're like... it's like Virtual Reality.

VR. Right.

A little later.

I'm stuffed. Let's pick up and move on.

Behind you!

Grrrrrrr!

Grab your weapons!

It's huge.

No time to waste.

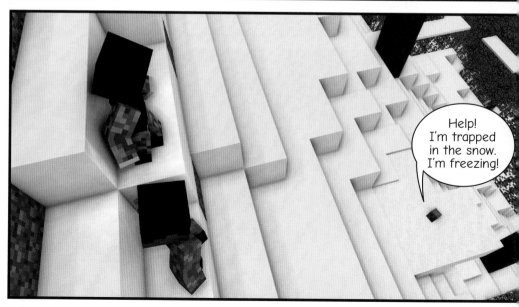

Chapter 6:
Hess

Well, we've had reports of six glitches so far, and they seem to be causing problems.

Six? I don't understand. That's not possible. We only created one glitch.

There was a glitch by my village and I'll tell you it's making some people very unhappy.

How did you link it to us?

When someone in my village reported seeing another glitch out on the plains, I came to look around. I found where you had lunch and where you destroyed that zombie. I saw you go up the mountain, so I followed you.

Can you show us what has everyone upset?

How far is your village?

Not far. Follow me.

several minutes later.

We got stuff!

I think that's it.

Okay, stand back. I'm going to flip this switch and the reverse glitch opefully should do the trick.

CLICK!

ZZZZZZ!

No more potatoes!

Ban Free Potatoes

No Free Potato

Hurray!

Not until we fix the other glitches.

So, can we make a list of where the other glitches are?

I said, not exactly.

Who told you about the glitches?

Not who, what.

The campfire told you?

Ooooh. Campfire signals. Like Morse code communication from other villages.

Yeah, smoke signals. We can create plumes of different sized smoke blobs in a special order and it's like sending a coded message. Any villager who can see the smoke plumes and knows the code can read it.

So we know the general areas where we saw the smoke signals, but that's it.

Hmm. I think I can make a glitch sensor to detect where a new glitch has occurred. It will need to be constructed somewhere in the nearby vicinity of the glitch.

Why?

The sensor needs to be placed close to quantum traces of the glitch in order to detect them.

To get to the general area, I think I can modify my original glitch contraption.

I'm going to need some more supplies. And we need to go back up the mountain.

Follow me.

CHAPTER 7:
GRAVEL

We're making maps?

Once these modded sensors and an observer detect the location of a current or past glitch, the circuitry and comparators inform the lectern, which translates coordinates to the cartography function.

Then the table pops out a map. The map helps us find the bunny glitch site.

Okay. You are a genius. I didn't understand anything but the word *bunny*. And I think you mean *killer* bunny.

Well, let's see if it works first.

CLICK.

No, just send them back to wherever they came from. Like the potatoes.

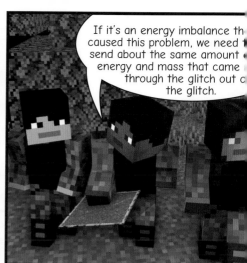

If it's an energy imbalance th caused this problem, we need send about the same amount energy and mass that came through the glitch out c the glitch.

Look. Gravel.

So what?

I want to get some flint so we can have a flint and steel. It's a good tool to have in our arsenal for making fire or lighting a portal or setting enemies on fire, or whatever. Plus, I need it if I need to make more arrows.

Good idea. We should all have a flint and steel.

Hold on. The gravel is collapsing!

FSFSFSSFS

CHAPTER 8: HUNGRY

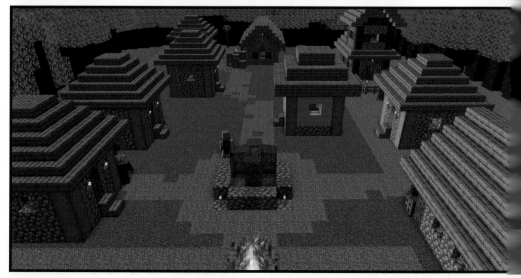

So how you two escape, Dward?

Ah the prison doors just sprung open all of a sudden and we booked it for the door.

This is a small rabbit. There's a whole buncha big nasty ones out there. Keep us fed for weeks.

And where'd you find such a big rabbit?

They're eating one of the killer bunnies.

I wonder how they caught it.

Probably how their friends caught us.

At least it bought us some time.

I don't think the villagers from the mansion recognized us.

I was hoping they would.

Yeah, and be really grateful we SAVED them and then save us in return.

Chapter 9: Hunt

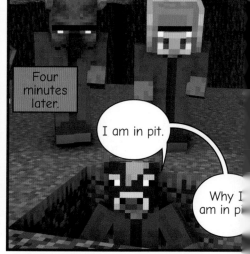

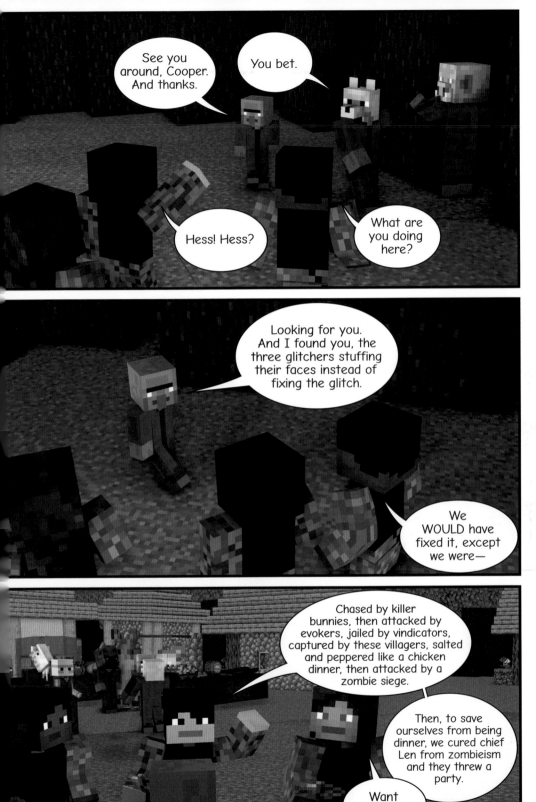

Sure. I didn't hear anything from you for over a day. So I decided to follow you and see what's what.

How'd you follow us?

I used your little glitch contraption.

What?

I watched you. Step in and press the button.

Okay.... I'm not sure that was a great idea, but....

So did you find out what the glitch was?

Giant rabbits' feet?

This is the way we get up to the canopy.

How do you find the bunnies from up here?

Those bunnies have got clompers you wouldn't believe. You can see their pawprints from up here.

So Hess, did you know about this village?

The village, yes. But not exactly where it was.

We heard that the illagers.... did experiments on them.

We went through the whole mansion. It was weird.

We were locked up there, too! Do you think they were going to... going to...

Probably.

Look! I see tracks there.

Come on!

Chapter 10:
Warren

I'm okay, but—
Oh no!

Quick!
Pull me up!

Aaaagh!

The rabbit's
got Hess!

ZING!

BONK!

I hit it, but it's not stopping!

Quick! Let's follow!

It's taking Hess back to the warren!

We've got to go in.

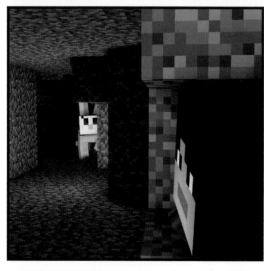

CHAPTER 11: EXTREMES

A little later.

Oh, bunnies...

You bad evil bunnies...

It's tasty Zed, strolling around in your warren.

⸦Eeeee!⸧

⸦Eeeeeee!⸧

⸦Eeeeee!⸧

⸦Eeeeee!⸧

They're coming!

⸦Eee!⸧

⸦EEEE⸧

⸦Eeeee!⸧

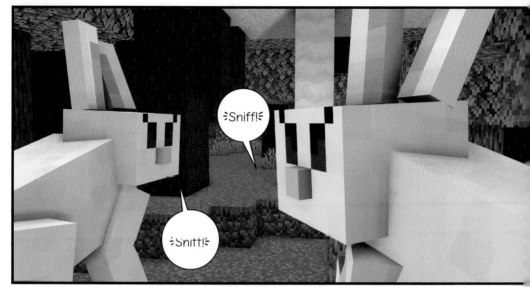

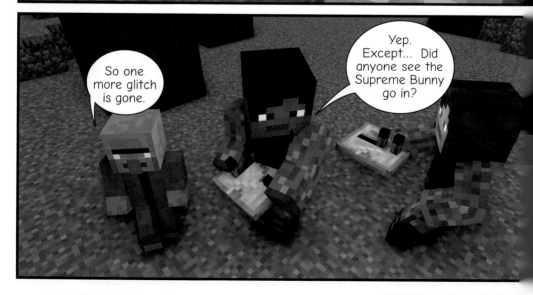

CHAPTER 12: BONFIRE